Thos. Ambrose Butler

The Irish on the Prairies

And Other Poems

Thos. Ambrose Butler

The Irish on the Prairies
And Other Poems

ISBN/EAN: 9783744677899

Printed in Europe, USA, Canada, Australia, Japan

Cover: Foto ©Thomas Meinert / pixelio.de

More available books at **www.hansebooks.com**

THE

IRISH ON THE PRAIRIES,

AND

OTHER POEMS.

BY

Rev. THOS. AMBROSE BUTLER,

NEW YORK:
D. & J. SADLIER & CO., 31 BARCLAY STREET.
MONTREAL:
Corner Notre-Dame and St. Francis Xavier Sts.
———
1874.

Entered according to Act of Congress, in the year 1873, by

THOS. AMBROSE BUTLER,

in the Office of the Litrarian of Congress, at Washington.

DEDICATED

TO

HIS FAITHFUL, LOVING FRIENDS

IN THE "OLD LAND"

AND

IN THE NEW

BY

THE AUTHOR.

PREFACE.

THE Author sends forth this little book of Poems, on its precarious journey, with no small amount of diffidence. It contains the simple fruits of many pleasant hours of literary labor in the bright domain of Poetry—hours in the years of youth and early manhood, and in the noon of life.

Some of the following Poems have already appeared in the Dublin "Nation," above the nom de plume "*Eblana;*" others are to be found in recent numbers of the New York "Emerald," and some have lately been inserted in numbers of "Irish Penny Readings." Many, however, have never, until now, been brought forth to seek the favor of the reading public. Amongst the latter is the principal poem of the volume—"The Irish on the Prairies."

The Author cherishes a hope that "The Irish on the Prairies" will be a welcome guest to the *exiles of Erin; will be deemed worthy of the place assigned to it as usher to the other Poems of the volume; will be found a faithful exponent of Irish feeling in the "Old Land" and the New; and a genuine index of the sentiments of a "Soggarth Aroon."*

Many of the minor Poems have been composed in the Author's lonely, happy home, beside an Irish chapel, in the shadows of the hills of Wicklow, where, as a "Country-Curate," the early years of his missionary life glided calmly along.

Some have been composed in the home of the exile, beside the rolling prairies of Kansas, in tranquil moments, after the busy priestly labors of the day.

Go forth, little book! into the wide world of Literature. May your simple pages bring brightness to the eyes of many exiles of Erin, and a gleam of sunshine to the hearts of loved ones far away.

T. A. B.

CATHEDRAL, LEAVENWORTH,
    KANSAS, *September,* 1873.

CONTENTS.

POEMS.

	PAGE
THE IRISH ON THE PRAIRIES:	
Part I.—Introductory	11
Part II.—New and Old	18
Our Future	44
The Exodus	47
The Nation's Muster-Roll	49
The Old Year	52
Avon-Liffey	55
The Lost Home	59
The Church	64
A Retrospect	67
The Birth of the Spring	70
Dreams	72
A Prison Scene	73
Glendalough	78
Elegy on my Sister	85
Commemoration Day	88
Godless Teachings	91
Doctor Yore	94

Contents.

	PAGE
Dalkey	97
Our University	103
Ode on Washington's Birth-Day	107
Winter in Town	110
A Prologue	111

SONGS.

The Wicklow Vales	117
The Dance	120
My Lovely Isle, Adieu!	122
Gazing Westward	124
O, Lovely Land!	126
Hunting Song	128
The Friends whom I Loved Long Ago	130
The Green Flag	131
"God Save Old Ireland"	133
There's Music midst the Mountains	136
Farewell, Dear Land!	138
Irish-American Brigade	140
The Hurlers	142
The Fiddler	145
From Far Away	147
The Little Bit of Land	149
Faithful unto Death	151
A Green Sod from Erin	153
The Exile's Love	155
Christmas on the Prairies	157
The Fenian Name	159
Farewell of the Irish Maiden	160

POEMS.

THE
Irish on the Prairies.

PART I.

INTRODUCTORY.

I.

COME, heap up the logs on the hearth-stone, and shut out the wintery blast;
To-night, in our snug little shanty, I'll tell you some tales of the Past.
And while the wind howls on the prairies, and drives the white snow to the door,
I'll visit in fancy the Old Land, and stand on her Emerald shore.
'Twill lift up a load from my old heart, and calm all my longings awhile,
To live o'er the Past, and to speak of the scenes of that beautiful isle.

'Twill cheer me to fill your young bosoms with
 love for the suffering land—
To make you feel proud of Old Erin, and ever
 her foemen withstand.

II.

The Old Land!—the Old Land! I love her,
 though naught of her form can be seen—
Though thousands of miles of the prairies and
 billowy seas intervene—
Though want and affliction surround her, and
 tyranny tramples her down,
And leaves her oppressed and dejected,—de-
 prived of her sceptre and crown.
Not thine is the fault, weeping Mother! thy chil-
 dren are leaving thy breast,
To seek o'er the billowy ocean a home in this
 land of the West.
Poor Queen! there are hearts that still love thee,
 and hands that would strike for thy fame,
Though traitors still fawn to the tyrants, and
 sycophants blush at thy name.

III.

Is Poverty hateful, degrading? Is Sorrow deserving of scorn?
Can man make you hate the Old Island—the land where your father was born?
Is false-hearted Britain so pow'rful, that far o'er the boisterous sea
The lies and the taunts that she utters reëcho midst homes of the free?
Is Freedom a phantom, delusion, to tempt the sad exile to roam
To climes where the sun-light of Justice shall never illumine his home?
Is man what his Maker intended, on mountain and prairie and plain—
As free as the winds of the heavens that sweep o'er the waves of the main?

IV.

But Patrick, my son! if they taunt you, and smile as they utter your name,
Forget not the Saint of my Country—rejoice in the light of his fame.

And tell to the scoffers the glories that shone
    on his banner of old,
When back from the skies of Old Ireland the
    darkness of Slavery roll'd.
When high on the green hills of Erin the ensign
    of Calvary rose,
An emblem of hope to the Christian, a sign of
    defeat to his foes,—
A banner we planted wherever the foot of an
    Irishman trod—
We march'd in the steps of Our Master—we
    fought the great battles of God!

V.

And Brigid, my darling! midst many the Faith
    of your Mother avow,
Nor suffer a blush for a Virgin to mantle your
    cheeks or your brow;
But proudly acknowledge Saint Brigid—"the
    Mary of Erin"—whose name
Was honor'd in ages departed, and shines through
    the annals of fame.
The lamp of the convent whose splendor beamed
    forth like a beautiful star,

Illuming the path of the maidens who came to
    her shrine from afar,—
Who came where the heart found a treasure that
    earth could not ever afford—
A gift that is offered by Heaven to virgins who
    follow the Lord!

VI.

Sweet love of our Faith and our Country!—for-
    ever unfading they last,
Like ivy-leaves twining together round desolate
    wrecks of the Past,—
Round abbeys whose gables have fallen,—round
    castles whose turrets are gone,—
Round towers that stand up majestic, in valleys
    deserted, alone,—
Round ruins of churches whose steeples oft
    echoéd the voice of the bell,
But totter'd and crumbl'd in tempests, and rang
    their own funeral-knell,
And mingled their dust with the valleys'—an
    emblem of patriots brave,
Who fall on the breast of their country, and find
    in its bosom a grave!

VII.

God's blessing be ever upon thee, my beautiful
  isle far away!
May tempests ne'er shatter thy beauty, may time
  never bring thee decay!
But ever be noble, though fallen, and ever be
  lovely, though lone—
If Mother of Sorrows yet smiling midst tears for
  her sons who are gone!
O! tyrants can never destroy thee! O! sorrows
  can never deface
The hope that has liv'd through the ages, and
  gladdened the suffering race;
Nor exile and happiness banish remembrance of
  days that have fled.
No! no!—by the Past and its sorrows! Ah!
  no, by the graves of the dead!

VIII.

My children! we fled from the famine—the evil
  that tyranny made,—
And exiles o'er seas and the prairies in search of
  some happiness stray'd.

We found it afar from Old Ireland ;—but often I
    think, with a sigh,
Far better to live in "the Old Land,"—far better
    in Erin to die!
To live on a little contented,—to manfully strug-
    gle awhile,—
To go to the grave of my fathers, and sleep in
    the Sanctified Isle.
Far sweeter to follow old customs, and live like
    our fathers of old,
Than wander a stranger midst peoples, and die
    in the struggle for gold!

IX.

But now let us heap up the fire-wood, and sit in
    the light of the blaze ;
The snow is still falling and drifting, and day-
    light in heaven decays ;
And everything seems to incite me to picture
    the Present and Past,—
The scenes in the Old Isle of Beauty, and here
    where my fortune is cast—
The contrast between home in Ireland and here
    in "the Land of Free,"—

Between the New World with its greatness, and
olden lands over the sea :
To show you why often at even' my mind seems
to wander astray—
My heart, like a bird in its prison, is throbbing
for Erin to-day!

PART II.

NEW AND OLD.

I.

AMERICA! Parent of Freemen! who once
as a giant arose,
And shook off the shackles of Britain, and scatter'd the merciless foes ;
Who summon'd the nations in bondage to come
to the home of the free—
From crumbling old kingdoms of Europe, from
suffering isles of the sea.
To come to the cities uprising on mountain and
valley and plain,
Beside the great lakes and the rivers, beside the
wild waves of the main.

To come to the prairies out-stretching for thousands of miles far away,
Where buffalo graze though the meadows, and timorous antelope stray.

II.

They answer the call of Columbia—gallant disciples of toil—
And Commerce is thron'd in the cities, and Labor is lord of the soil.
And under "the Star-spangled Banner" the native and foreigner stand,
As noble Apostles of Freedom and props of the prosperous land.
And grand is the stride of the nation in all that exalts and redeems,
And joyous the face of her children, enliven'd by Liberty's beams.
And newness and freshness surround her, unlike the Old Country's decay.
The night of her bondage is over—she woke to a happier day!

III.

How youthful the nation appeareth, wherever the wanderer goes!
How strong while the stream of new people, like blood through her arteries flows!
How new to the eye of the Exile the face of the cities that rise
With magical force from the forests and lift their young heads to the skies!
No sign of antiquity near them; no ruins of castle or hall;
No palace of baron or tyrant; no ivy-clad tottering wall;
No mark to betray to the passer the dwelling of sorrow and care;
No sign of oppression, for Poverty stalks not the streets in despair!

IV.

Away midst the flow'rs of the prairies, beside the green woods of the West,
"The Settler" is raising his cabin,—the red-bird is building her nest,

Where naught of the noise of the cities, or breath of its tumult or strife,
Can reach to the ear of the peasant, or ripple the stream of his life.
E'en there, midst the oldest of forests, the newness of life can be seen,—
E'en there is the foot-print of Freedom, where trail of the savage has been,—
E'en there, far away from his kindred, the Exile from Erin appears,
With hopes, reawak'd in his bosom, that slumber'd in gloomier years.

V.

My children!—the home of my fathers—the spot where my being began—
The scenes of my youthful affection—how fair to the vision of man!
The cot on the hill, midst the hedges, whose walls were as white as the snow—
The valleys, with vesture of verdure, where silvery rivulets flow!
The meadows, where "butter-cups" mingle with " daisies" at birth of the May,--

The woods, where the black-birds are piping
    their notes through the length of the day,—
The mountains, in majesty standing, as sentinels
    guarding the vales,
With brows that are furrow'd by streamlets, and
    wrinkl'd by wintery gales!

VI.

Out here on the beautiful prairies the scene is
    delightfully grand,
For signs of the richest fertility cover the face
    of the land,
And waves of the brightest of verdure are roll-
    ing forever amain,
When Winter releases the meadows, and lifts up
    his garb from the plain.
But *sameness* of scene is before us; for Nature,
    though lavish of stores,
Bestow'd not the gift of variety found on "the
    Emerald shores."
But far through the boundless dominions a prai-
    rie, or forest, appears,
As changeless in form as the ocean that roll'd
    through the thousands of years.

VII.

Around on "the Settlement" gazing, the Exile can never behold
A scene to remind him of Erin—a home like his fathers of old:
The hedges of hawthorn and sallow—the furze, with its yellowish flow'r—
The trees that are standing majestic, by hillock and cottage and bower.
Ah, no! We have left them forever, and rude are the dwellings we see—
The huts of the logs of the forests, of branches of many a tree,
And rough are the fences surrounding the confines of many a home.
O! naught like the hedges of Ireland we find wheresoever we roam!

VIII.

'Tis true in our home on the prairies we've plenty, we've riches in store,—
'Tis true that the tyrannous "*Agent*" can threaten my people no more,—

'Tis true that the land that we toil on is ours'
    and our children's alone,
And free on the soil of the freeman we're rich as
    a king on his throne.
But O! how I long for the laughter that rose
    round my home far away;
The music of mirth that was swelling by fire-
    sides at close of the day;
The jokes and the tales of the neighbors, whom
    sorrows could never o'erthrow.
Ah! here the heart's music is wanting we heard
    in the years long ago!

IX.

When Summer goes over the waters and smiles
    on our Emerald Queen,
How lovely the look of the valleys! how pleas-
    ant each sun-lighted scene!
How cheering at mid-day to wander adown by
    the meadows and streams,
Not dreading the sun in the heavens, but loving
    the glance of his beams.
For never, as here on the prairies, does sun-light
    oppress or destroy;

It smiles and it dances in Erin—it lights up the
  spirits with joy.
And welcome, as flowers of the May-time, is
  Summer all over our isle ;
For man, like the flow'rs of the valleys, revives
  in the light of its smile.

X.

What sports we enjoy'd in the meadows, when
  labor had ceas'd for the day !
What joy and excitement apparent, when "hurl-
  ers" prepared for their play !
What lively emotions, as onward the strugglers
  to victory sped !
Ah ! where are the friends of my boyhood ? I
  sigh for the years that have fled.
I sigh ! for my wealth cannot purchase such joy
  as I felt long ago :
The peace of the poorest of peasants—the calm
  that the rich never know.
I sigh on the breast of the prairies, and pray
  that kind Heaven may smile
On homes and the hearts of my people who
  dwell in the Emerald Isle.

XI.

Alas! I can never recall them—the scenes 'neath the shadowing trees—
The light-hearted "Piper," whose music arose on the wings of the breeze;
The men and the maidens who joyously join'd in the dance on "the Green,"
And danc'd till the sun-light departed, and darkness came down on the scene.
But hold! I will sing you a ditty—a song of the Dance in the Glen!
To lilt a sweet air of my country will cheer up my spirits again.
So stir the red-logs and be silent, or join in the chorus with me;
We'll joyfully sing of the customs of father-land over the sea.

THE DANCE.

[AIR—Billy O'Rourke ma bouchal.]

THE Summer-sun is laughing down,
 And o'er the heather glancing;
We'll haste away ere close of day,
 To join the peasants dancing

Beneath the ivy-clothed trees
   That guard the farmer's dwelling,
And softly shake their leafy bells,
   While music's strains are swelling.
We'll haste away, we'll haste away,
   Along the scented heather;
We'll join the merry peasant band,
   And "trip the sod" together.

From silent glen, from mossy moor,
   From cabin lone and dreary,
They come—the friezed and hooded band,
   With spirits never weary.
With hearts so light that sorrows ne'er
   Can break their sense of pleasure—
The Irish heart that laughs at care
   Is bless'd with brightest treasure.
We'll haste away, we'll haste away,
   Along the scented heather;
We'll join the merry peasant band,
   And "trip the sod" together.

The stars will peep amidst the trees,
   Their light with moonbeams blended,

Before the music dies away,
    Before the dance is ended.
And joke and laughter, wild and free,
    Ring round the farmer's dwelling,
And lithesome limbs keep measur'd time
    Where Irish airs are swelling.
We'll haste away, we'll haste away,
    Along the scented heather;
We'll join the merry peasant band,
    And "trip the sod" together.

As long as happy Irish hearts
    Are throbbing through the Nation—
As long as Ireland's exiled sons
    Are found on God's creation—
As long as Music's thrilling strains
    Can wake a sweet emotion,
We'll save the customs of our sires,
    At home and o'er the ocean.
We'll haste away, we'll haste away,
    Along the scented heather;
We'll join the merry peasant band,
    And "trip the sod" together.

XII.

But ah! in our home on the prairies, when day
    has arrived at its close,
The toiler is worn with his labor—the weari'd is
    wanting repose.
Forever, forever so eager to gather the wealth
    that deprives
The heart of its lightness and brightness, and
    darkens the path of our lives.
O! brighter the hut of the poorest, wherever
    contentment is seen,
Than dwellings where trouble is brooding—the
    palace of chieftain or queen.
And sweeter to live in the Present, than wander
    in thought far way,
Nor wish for a gleam of the Future, but live in
    the light of To-day.

XIII.

No music is heard in our shanty, no music is
    heard on the plain,
No music amidst the wild forests, where silence
    and solitude reign.

No notes but the lays of the songsters—the birds
    in the Spring of the year,—
In days when the Summer is reigning, and
    flow'rs in the valleys appear.
No piper e'er plays on the prairies, no peasants
    e'er dance in the glen,
No maidens of Erin e'er warble the songs of their
    childhood again,
But sit in the shade of their dwellings when
    Summer-sun sinks to his rest,
And sigh for the beautiful Summer that smiles
    on "the Land of the West!"

XIV.

The Sunday!—how welcome in Erin!—how
    happy, how blest is the day!
The dawn of its morning seemed ever to drive
    the dark sorrows away.
And even in wildest of weather, when Winter
    was roughest of mien,
The Angel of Peace was beside us, and smiled
    on the gloomiest scene.
And like to the voice of the Seraphs, who sang
    to the shepherds of old,

The bell of the church in the village its musical
    melody roll'd,—
A voice to awaken devotion—a summons to
    haste to the shrine,
And kneel at the foot of the altar, to worship
    the Master Divine!

XV.

From many a home on the mountains, from
    many a hut in the glen,
From many a cot in the valleys there came forth
    a streamlet of men:
The young in their spring of existence, the old
    in their time of decay,
Went forth in the light of the Sunday to haste
    to the chapel to pray.
The agéd, with tottering footsteps, with eager-
    ness moved in the throng;
The young, in the flush of their vigor, proceeded
    with swiftness along.
And like to the rivulets spreading in streams o'er
    the breast of the land,
The maidens and boys of the parish out-spread
    into many a band.

XVI.

The Chapel!—the old parish Chapel!—ah! fondly my fancy recalls
The form that it ever presented—the hue of its mouldering walls;
The quaint-looking windows and arches, the tow'r where the cross was display'd;
The statue of Joseph the Patron, and Mary—Immaculate Maid.
The font where the worshippers halted to sprinkle their brow, and to pray
A blessing on home and its people, and peace through the sanctified day.
The porch where we enter'd how sombre!—the altar how simple and bright!
It gladden'd the heart of the wearied, and fill'd the devout with delight.

XVII.

Not far from the old parish Chapel, and nigh to a sheltering wood,
The mould'ring remains of an abbey in tottering majesty stood.

The ivy was over the ruins—the freshness of life
    with decay—
The ivy will flourish for ages, the walls will soon
    moulder away!
Around are the graves of our fathers—they sleep
    in the sanctified dust,
With the Saints and the Martyrs beside them—
    the bones of beatified just.
They sleep where no sorrows can reach them,
    and under the Emerald sod;
They rest 'neath the grass of Old Ireland, and
    near to the temple of God.

XVIII.

Ah! oft, ere the bell of the chapel had summon'd
    the people to pray,
I've sat midst the tombs of the vanish'd, or
    join'd with the children in play;
Or listen'd with boyish emotion to patriot spirits
    who told
Of hopes in the future of Ireland—her struggles,
    her sorrows of old.
Or heard the fond parent relating the news from
    his sons o'er the sea,—

From homes on the breast of the prairies—from
    lands where his children are free,
Till, stirr'd by the words of the speakers, my
    spirits in tumult arose,
With love for the land of my fathers, with hate
    for her merciless foes!

XIX.

Loud sounded the bell in the turret,—"his Rev-
    'rence" appeared on the way—
The Speakers retir'd to the chapel—the little
    ones ceas'd from their play;
And hearts that had sorrow'd a moment, and
    lips that had spoken of pain,
Were moved by the voice of Religion, and la-
    bor'd for heaven again.
And earth and its cares were forgotten, and hope
    of a future above
Arose midst the lights of the altar that typify
    Catholic love:
The love that no gloom can extinguish, no
    tyrant of earth can destroy,
That cheers the fond heart of the mother, and
    follows her wandering boy.

XX.

The mothers! the poor Irish mothers!—ah! many have wept by the shore,
And sobb'd as they parted from children—the lov'd who will see them no more.
And many have borne through the future a wound that no science could heal—
A wound that is like to heart-breaking, that none but a mother can feel!
How many have found naught to comfort, no solace their trouble to calm,
No hope through the length of existence to pour o'er their spirits a balm,
But that which the faith of our Fathers and Christ in His temple afford—
The faith and the hope of a meeting beside the great throne of the Lord?

XXI.

There's solace when under "The Stations" the mothers in solitude pray,
And follow, in spirit, "The Mother and Son" on "the dolorous way;"

And mingle their sorrows with Mary's, and stand
    by Her under the Cross,
And fill'd with the thought of Her dolors, forget,
    for a moment, their loss.
Forget all the world, and the troubles that darken the pathway of years;
Remain in the gloom of the Passion, and give to
    the Saviour their tears;
Then offer the loss of their children a sacrifice
    up to the Son,
While praying the will of the Father, not theirs',
    may for ever be done!

XXII.

But here, in the wilds of the prairies, the Sunday
    no joyousness brings—
No heart, like a lark in the morning, with feeling
    of happiness sings;
No dawning of hope with the daybreak to souls
    that are panting with love,
That thirst for a drop from the fountains that
    spring in the Kingdom above.
No music of bells from a distance—no crowds of
    "parishioners" pass,

And offer a glad salutation as onward they haste to "the Mass;
Or come with us back from the chapel, and sit for awhile in our cot,—
Ah, friends still at home in Old Ireland! how sadly I envy your lot!

XXIII.

The Sunday arrives with its silence. No labor of sinewy hand—
No sound of the axe in the forests—no plough in the bountiful land;
But rest in the home of the exile—a rest for the body alone!
The mind is as active as ever—it flieth to days that have flown.
A chapel—"a church," as *they* call it—is many a mile to the west,—
Within it the birds of the prairies in Winter have shelter and rest.
No voice to disturb them at morning—no bell-tones to scare them away;
For seldom the priest can attend us, and stand at the altar to pray.

XXIV.

The church on the breast of the prairies—how
    humble, how shatter'd, how lone!
Its frame-work is warping and rotting—the grass
    on its pathway has grown.
Its roof in the Winter is clothed with snow, that
    unmelting remains
As long as the drifts in the forests, or flakes on
    the face of the plains;
For seldom the breath of the fire-wood is felt
    through the cold of the year,
And seldom in Winter our footprints upon the
    white pathway appear.
Alone! all alone on the prairies! alone on the
    sanctified ground!
Ah no! for invisible angels are hovering ever
    around!

XXV.

The altar! Ah! think of the manger—the cra-
    dle where Jesus was laid
That morning when angels of beauty stood
    round the Immaculate Maid.

Ah! think of the crib and the stable, and starlight that fell on the floor!
Respect the low shrine on the prairies, and blush at its poorness no more.
Ah! not a fond thought of Old Ireland the altar-piece ever recalls;
No church on the prairies presents us the hue of the mouldering walls
Of chapels that stand in the valleys, where streams through the fatherland flow—
O God! for one hour in the chapel where oft I have prayed long ago!

XXVI.

On Sundays when Mass is expected, the settlers, at dawning of day,
Are seen in the woods on the prairies, that lie from the church far away.
They come in their lumbering wagons, their little ones seated a-near,
At times when the Summer is smiling, and often in "Fall" of the year;
But seldom, when Winter is howling, the wagons are seen on the plain;

At home by the stove in the shanty, the mother
    and children remain.
And seldom a worshipper walketh to Mass as
    they do in *our land*,—
We miss the bright streamlets of peasants, we
    meet not a juvenile band.

XXVII.

No crowds in the shades of the chapel—no little
    ones running around ;
No tombs midst the trees in the valley to tell of
    the sanctified ground ;
No "Soggarth" like him whom we honored as
    "father" in Erin of old,
Whose voice on the altar was pleasant as ring
    of the purest of gold !
'Tis true that we honor our Pastors, whatever
    the land of their birth,—
'Tis true that we worship our Maker wherever
    His temple on earth ;
But O ! what a joy to the Irish—to exiles what
    heavenly boon !
To hear in the church on the prairies the voice
    of their "Soggarth aroon !"

XXVIII.

No fount with its water so holy is found in the
    Winter-time there,
For sprinkling the brow ere the worshipper en-
    ters the temple of prayer.
No "spring" on the hill-side is bubbling — no
    "wells" that are blest can be seen,
Like those that are holy in Ireland, and sprinkle
    her garment of green:
The "wells" where the pilgrims are halting and
    sad ones are seeking relief,
Where sick ones are freed from their troubles,
    and cur'd by the strength of belief—
By faith such as faith is in Erin—the faith that
    no pow'r could destroy—
That lives in the hearts of our people, and lights
    the lone cabin with joy!

XXIX.

O! often in slumbers of midnight I dream of my
    isle o'er the sea,
And see her all radiant with beauty—the home
    of the happy and free.

And often I dream that the island is like to a
 barque far away—
A green-painted ship that will reach us before
 the first dawn of the day.
O God! if the waves could upheave her and bear
 her in majesty o'er,
To rest in the sunlight of Freedom beside the
 American shore ;
Or if this invincible nation would wrench her
 from tyranny's chain,
Then, then I would fly to Old Ireland, and rest
 on her bosom again.

XXX.

My children! mayhap in the future, beside this
 lone home in the West,
Some heart-broken exiles of Erin may seek for a
 shelter and rest,
Some other lone wanderers settle on prairies as
 rich as our own,
Till round on the wild a New Ireland of beauty
 and pow'r shall have grown.
Then down in the woods in the even' the voice
 of the village shall ring—

Then out on the prairies the maidens the songs
of Old Erin shall sing—
Then sports that we lov'd in Old Ireland shall
rise up again to the view,
And plant all the joys of "the Old Land" amidst
the bright scenes of "the New."

XXXI.

O Patrick in heaven! smile ever adown on my
isle far away!
O follow the steps of the exiles wherever through
life they may stray!
O guard the bright treasure and freedom you
gave to our fathers of yore,
Till steps of your soldiers shall echo in triumph
on every shore!
O aid us to struggle forever for honors no tyrants
can claim,
Till Erin shall rise from her sorrows, and nations
shall honor her name.
Then, then will her children, uprising on moun-
tain and prairie and plain,
With joy rush to Erin, their Mother, to make her
a Nation again!

Our Future.

I.

A MOMENT we rest on our voyage of sorrow,
    Afar on the waters of fugitive Time,
And hope that the light that will herald the morrow
    May show us the shores of some beautiful clime.
That shadows, now dark'ning the billows before us,
    May fade on the rim of the waters afar,
And clouds, that are sailing in majesty o'er us,
    May sink in the light of some glittering star!

II.

Oh, Ireland! how often thy patriot spirits
    Have look'd for a day when thy sorrows would cease—

Have long'd for the boon which the freeman inherits—
 Have pray'd, midst their tears, for thy happy release—
Have sent forth their hopes, like the dove o'er the billows,
 But homeward they came with no branch of the palm.
They found but the seed of the dark weeping-willows—
 No rest mid the waters—no promise of calm!

III.

The Future,—in fancy I seek to behold it;
 To look on the signs that will usher its reign;
To gaze through the shadows that thickly enfold it;
 To view all the scenes that will come in its train;
To look to the land where our childhood was cherished,
 To try if her glory will glisten again;
If Liberty's soul mid her ruins has perished—
 Mid ruins of dwellings and corses of men.

IV.

Oh! think will the flocks of the stranger be straying
  Along by the valleys where hamlets have been;
Will shepherds, alone, by the streamlets be playing
  The pipe that once gather'd a crowd to the green;
Will Celts in the land of adoption be reaping
  A harvest of glory in battle's career,
Whilst far on the shores where their fathers are sleeping
  No marks of their march or their struggle appear!

V.

I know not,—but often I think, with a feeling
  Of sadness that borrows a pang from the past,
How silently forward the Future is stealing,
  Whilst men in our isle are in lethargy cast.
In gloomiest season how cheering and pleasant

To scatter the seeds of the flow'rs for the May!
The Future will tread in the track of the Present:
Then, brothers, prepare for her coming to-day.

The Exodus.

I.

THEY are going, they are going where Missouri's waves are flowing,
  Where the waving crops are growing for the tiller of the soil;
Where the light of Justice beameth, and the sword of Justice gleameth,
  And good fortune ever seemeth as attendant upon toil.

II.

Far from Erin they are flying where their fathers' bones are lying,
  Where Atlantic's waves are sighing 'round her desolated shore;

Where the streams of care are welling 'round
    each simple peasant's dwelling,
  And the bravest hearts are swelling with the
    sorrow at their core.

III.

There are parents fond, endearing; there are
    scenes yet bright and cheering;
  But an evil star is peering o'er the dwellings
    of our isle—
O'er the cot amidst the bushes, where the shining river rushes,
  Where the sparkling fountain gushes like a
    heart that has no guile.

IV.

They are leaving home for ever; and the fondest kindred sever;
  And the light of joy shall never brightly beam
    upon their breast;
Though the freeman's flag is o'er them, and a
    life of peace before them,
  Yet the mother fond who bore them sighs
    with sorrow in the West.

V.

Let them go! may Heaven speed them! be a
 blessed lot decreed them;
But if Ireland e'er shall need them, may they
 hasten o'er the sea;
May the loving hearts that slumbered, by the
 weight of grief encumbered,
Beat for Erin's woes unnumbered, and return
 to set her free!

The Nation's Muster-Roll.
(*The Irish Census of 1861.*)

I.

BEHOLD our Nation's muster-roll to-day—
 Oh! how it tells her sad and fallen state!
Not midst her foes in dreadful battle fray,
 Did Erin's children meet the soldier's fate,
Nor yet as beggars at their master's gate;
 But, proudly scorning Ireland's hated foe,
They left the land—in exiled homes to wait
 For better days, to strike a gallant blow
  Upon their native fields, where Shannon's
   waters flow.

II.

But oh! for words to rouse the dying fire
  Of Celtic love for happy hearts at home!
To boldly wake the bard's majestic lyre,
  Till hearts would throb within their living dome!
Till now awhile our thoughts would sadly roam
  To scenes where shatter'd dwellings lowly lie:
And then to feel the tempest's blinding foam—
  To hear the winds of poignant sorrow sigh,
  Till men would start with rage, and join in Freedom's cry!

III.

Aye, men! the wreck will tell the tempest's force—
  The *pilot's* guile, or *pirate's* bloody sway—
The broken gables mark the spoiler's course,
  And give the lie to cringing slaves who say
That Erin's millions gather wealth to-day.
  The lordly prosper—peasants leave the land—
And thus, through cycles, Ireland's hopes decay:

Each tide of time that strikes the rugged strand,
  Sweeps off the country's wealth—the strong, the helping hand.

IV.

But cease to grieve—Jehovah loves our isle,
  Where faith has shone undimm'd amidst the gloom—
Where hope and love have sought His cheering smile,
  Whilst seated watching nigh the Nation's tomb.
Oh! soon will break, like summer's virgin bloom,
  A gleam of glory o'er our isle's expanse,
And chase the shades that far before us loom,
  And wake the Celt from out his heavy trance,
  To view the Nation's rise, and hail her bold advance.

The Old Year.

I.

AH! the Year has just departed, like a parent broken-hearted,
   When her once sweet-smiling children have been gathered to the clay.
In the Winter's gloom appalling, when the flaky snow is falling,
   And the earth's great heart is hardened, and her grassy head is gray.

II.

Nature seems o'ercome with sadness, and she feels no throb of gladness,
   When the laughing Sun at mid-day maketh diamonds of the snow!
And the voice of lamentation spreads across this wide creation,
   When the wild winds, moving onward, with a moaning accent blow.

III.

Lo! the icy tears are pendant from the turret-tops resplendent,
    And the branches of the poplars raise the morning plumes on high!
And the streams no longer hasten, roaring from the rocky basin,
    For the ice has stopp'd their wailings, and the bosoms cease to sigh!

IV.

Dead Year!—in Spring-time's splendor, when thy heart was soft and tender,
    Then fond Nature ope'd her treasures—fragrant odors for thy shrine—
And poor, weary mortals bless'd thee, whilst the beauteous Spring caress'd thee,
    And they hoped for more successors of so prosperous a line.

V.

Later on thy path of duty, when the Summer beamed in beauty,
    And the sunshine danced around thee, like a truant child at play—

When the brilliant sky of heaven smiled upon thee in the even',
  Then thou seemed to wish to mingle all the shades of night with day.

VI.

But the voice of death was calling when the Autumn leaves were falling,
  And the rustling withered leaflets sung the dirge before thy death,
And the clouds were edged with mourning when the shades of eve returning,
  Cast their gloom upon Creation as all Nature held its breath.

VII.

Soon thy parent, Time, forsook thee, and death at length o'ertook thee,
  And amidst the midnight shadows thou wast borne to thy tomb,
And poor mortals missed thee sadly; whilst old Time, careering gladly,
  Brought another New Year smiling from amidst the Winter's gloom.

Avon-Liffey.

I.

DOWN by the silent glades,
　Under the forest's shades,
Ever the glassy stream glideth along.
　Out in its rural space,
　Bright in its placid face,
Like a sweet spirit that knoweth no wrong!

II.

　See! how the willows bend,
　Hailing their olden friend;
Lo! how the lilies are sprinkled with spray!
　Downward they bend awhile,
　As when in sacred aisle
People are bless'd by the priest as they pray.

III.

　See how the waters sweep
　Down to the "Salmon Leap,"

Eagerly rushing, like children, to play.
    Oh! how they dance about,
    Raising a joyous shout,
Leaping the rugged rocks—gliding away.

IV.

    See yonder truant tide
    Seeking the rocky side,
Where, like a gem, the mill crowneth the hill;
    Down to the foaming wheel
    Softly the waters steal—
Laughing they roll it around as they will.

V.

    Onward the waters go,
    Down to the bed below,
Where the white foam saileth ever around—
    Stop not to sigh or breathe,
    Snatch but a foamy wreath,
Emblem of glory that mortals have found!

VI.

    Far from each sylvan scene,
    Far from the valleys green,

Far from the odors of garden and mead,
    Soon tow'rds the city's hum
    Onward the waters come—
On to Eblana they joyously speed.

VII.

    Look through the murky haze,
    Hiding the ancient days,
On through a hundred of decades of years,
    Where o'er the rolling main
    Hasten'd the pirate Dane—
Lo! on the Liffey his banner appears!

VIII.

    Later the tears of slaves
    Dropp'd in the silver waves;
Liffey look'd red as it swept through the vale:
    Blood of the Celtic race
    Fell o'er its placid face—
Ah! how they triumph'd, the Lords of the Pale!

IX.

    Oft rang the Abbey-bells*
    Out from the holy cells,

Over the water at Angelus' hour;
    Lo! as the music floats,
    Monks in the fishing-boats
Pray to their Patroness—speak of her pow'r.

X.

    Gone are the olden times,
    Lost, like the Abbey's chimes—
Crumbl'd the human clay, chieftains and slaves.
    Yet, midst the ages' flight,
    Constant as Truth and Right,
Rolls Avon-Liffey to Ocean's blue waves.

---

* Saint Mary's Abbey, Dublin. Leave was granted to the monks of this abbey, in the year 1185, to have fishing-boats on the waters of the Avon-Liffey.

The Lost Home.

I.

COME sit, my son, beneath the shade where Autumn winds are sighing;
The shadows, creeping down the woods, announce that day is dying;
And far the murky clouds out-spread—the floating flags of warning—
Where Alleghanies' giant hills were seen at early morning.

II.

Behold! my son, the fertile fields, where golden grain is swelling;
And far away the crested pines thy brother's axe is felling;
And yonder see our cheerful cot beside the mountain river,—
Thy father knows no master here but God, the mighty Giver.

III.

In other days, when life was young, and hope
    was beaming o'er me,
I lov'd my father's natal cot—I lov'd the isle
    that bore me,
And love it still—the dear old land—though
    ocean's waves divide us;
The thoughts of old and fancy's spell shall bring
    it shores beside us.

IV.

Oh! land of sorrows, Innisfail! the saddest, still
    the fairest!
Though ever-fruitful are thy breasts—though
    green the garb thou wearest,
In vain thy children seek thy gifts, and fondly
    gather round thee;
They live as strangers midst thy vales since dark
    oppression bound thee.

V.

My natal home beside the glen! how could I
    cease to love thee?
The yellow thatch was o'er thy walls,—the
    beeches wav'd above thee;

Thy sides were like the sea-gull's wings—of
purest, snowy brightness;
They woo'd the Sun, till round thy porch he
flung his silv'ry brightness.

VI.

Methinks I now behold thy smoke ascend from
yonder thicket—
Methinks I see my agéd sire beside thy open
wicket,
And hear my brothers' notes of mirth along the
valleys ringing,
Where maidens o'er the milking-pails the rural
songs are singing.

VII.

Around thy hearth, at day's decline, arose the
voice of gladness—
The fleeting years, as on they sped, flung in no
seeds of sadness;
And though the swelling tide of care oft roll'd
its waves beside us,
We clung in hope around our home—no perils
could divide us.

VIII.

But ah! on sudden, Famine's breath brought direful desolation;
Whilst tyrants cast their cruel laws around the dying nation,
And spurn'd the wasting, wither'd poor, for help, for mercy crying,—
The Saxons smil'd with joy to hear that Celtic sons were dying.

IX.

My God, it came!—the fearful gale—against our happy dwelling;
We stood the fearful shock awhile, though waves of care were swelling;
Whilst, like a monster midst the deep, which loves the tempest's thunder,
The lord who own'd our lands desir'd to see us sinking under.

X.

In vain the hopes we fed awhile! in vain each dear endeavor!
My father's fathers' natal home was lost to us for ever;

And cozy roof, and porch, and walls, were cast
    to earth together,
And we, in woe, were forced to face the Winter's
    direful weather.

XI.

Alanna! 'neath their native soil my parents'
    hearts are sleeping—
Across their lonely grassy graves the shamrock
    leaves are creeping;
And we are here amidst those wilds, where
    tyrants ne'er can bind us,
With lands as fertile—not so fair—as those
    we've left behind us.

XII.

Yes; true, my son! thy father dear has drunk
    the bitter potion;
Yet often midst those lonely woods he thinks
    with fond emotion,
That yonder billows seek our isle—that gentle
    zephyrs fan her:
Oh! may her exiles seek her, too, to raise her
    drooping banner!"

The Church.

I.

OLDEST rock amidst the waters! boldly bearest thou thy brow!
As in ages long forgotten, still unchanged thou standest now!
And the tempests waste their fury when they strike against thy side,
And the wild waves, leaping at thee, fall in drops into the tide.
Still they roll in times of storms when a mist is o'er the skies,
And thy face seems dark with sadness, and the raven round thee flies!
But forever shall thy bold front be as changeless as to-day,
Still as fearless in the tempest, and as firm amidst the spray.

II.

Grandest giant of the waters! on thy head a gem was set,
In thy days of early childhood, and it rests upon thee yet.
Yet undimmed its pristine splendor, but increasing through the years,
As the Sun, uprising slowly, with increasing light appears!
And that gem e'er sparkles brightly—nations in its beams behold
Brilliant beacon-lights of promise, like the Magis' star of old.
But never for one moment shall its brightness leave thy head
Until time's swift course is finished, and the race of man is dead.

III.

Oh! the Rock!—the Rock of Ages—which so proudly shows its form!
Which yet towers above the billows and defies the raging storm,

Is the rock the Saviour promised when He preached in Galilee,
Where His sheep would find a shelter, where His Prince would fix His See.
And the gem upon its summit, sparkling through the lapse of time,
Is the glorious Church of ages—light of life to every clime.
Like a star above the waters, peering through the world's foam !
Gem undimmed, on Rock of Ages is the holy Church of Rome.

IV.

Winds of discord ! strike ye strongly at the turret-headed Rock !
Sea of troubles ! pour your waters with a thunder-roaring shock !
Vain shall ever be your efforts ; God is ever still the same,
And the justice of Jehovah shall illumine Pio's name.
Nations ! come ye with your legions ! place your sentinels around !

Halt in haste! but tramp not proudly on the
　　consecrated ground!
God is watching o'er His temple—God is smiling
　　on our Pope;
And the Cross—the Christian's ensign—is the
　　Pontiff's flag of hope.

A Retrospect.

I.

THROUGH the solemn forest wending,
　　When the shades of eve are blending,
　　　With the hues the leaflets pendent
　　Fling along the shady way;
Oft we gaze, with growing sadness,
Tow'rds the lovely scenes of gladness
　　　That we left behind forever
　　At the dawning hour of day.

II.

Ah! 'tis thus when life is fading,
When the gloom of care is shading
　　　Many vistas bright and pleasant
　　Where our early life appears,

Oft we gaze awhile with sorrow
Which no moment's pang can borrow
 From our darksome life at present
 Back to scenes of vanish'd years.

III.

Oft has hope appear'd awaking
When the light of Knowledge breaking
 Waken'd Erin's fallen children
 From their dreams of want and woe.
When the bard, with truth and boldness,
Strove to chase the nation's coldness
 With his burning words of beauty,
 Like his brothers 'long ago.

IV.

Ah! the days of pleasant seeming
When our peasant bands were streaming,
 Like the mountain-rills unnumber'd,
 Down the hills, along the vales;
Rushing round, where, proudly soaring
High in hope, a chief was pouring
 Words of warning, words of promise,
 Hush'd ere long by Famine wails!

V.

Then the hopes awhile awoken,
Ere the island's heart was broken—
    Hopes in deeds of gallant daring
  Wrought by men of Irish mould,
Then the dreadful desolation
Sweeping o'er our trodden nation—
    Famine made by foreign masters,
  With the hellish craft of old!

VI.

Brothers! light may break to-morrow
O'er our gloomy path of sorrow.
    Look with hope across the ocean—
  Irish courage still remains.
O! "the green" is proudly waving
O'er the exiles, battles braving,
    Hoping still they yet may gather
  Nigh their foes on Irish plains!

The Birth of the Spring.

I.

Hush! our Mother Earth is waking; purple light is softly breaking
  Through the passing clouds that Winter fleeing bringeth in her train.
Smiling Spring! awake in beauty; pay to Time a daughter's duty;
  Wield thy magic wand of splendor o'er Creation's broad domain.

II.

Tempests wild—the Winter's vassals—sweeping round the proudest castles,
  Shouting, screaming forth their war-cry, struck the hearts of men with fear;
Bent the forest-lords before them, as they swept in fury o'er them,
  As they sent through leafless branches, triumph's wild, terrific cheer.

III.

Now the Winter's reign is ended. Queenly Spring her way has wended
  Down the hills whose brows are furrow'd by the rapid streamlet's waves,—
Down along the wrinkl'd valleys; through the silent, rural alleys;
  O'er the garden's swelling bosoms, to the vanish'd flow'rets' graves.

IV.

She will pour her balm around her, till the deadly chill that bound her,
  Shall in misty vapor vanish midst the fleeting Winter-clouds;
She will guard their tender childhood in the silent vale and wild-wood;
  She will wrap their heads at morning in the glist'ning dewy shrouds!

V.

O'er the bursting blossoms bending, she will woo the light descending
  From the throne of dazzling glory where the Sun in splendor reigns;

Midst her peaceful haunts delaying, through her
    bright dominions straying,
  Light of day will fondly linger, bound by
    Beauty's golden chains!

Dreams.

I.

HEED them not—the fleeting shadows float-
    ing through the midnight dreams,
Like the scenes that seem so pleasant 'neath the
    glassy-bosom'd streams:
Shining brightly, jewel-studded, 'neath the sil-
    ver-headed spray,—
Dreams—the phantom-works of Fancy—fade as
    night before the day.

II.

Heed them not—the shores of dreamland—trust
    no treasure to the ships
Sailing down the stream of Visions, midst the
    mighty mind's eclipse.

Trust no syren voice that rises where the misty shadows play.
Dreams—the phantom-works of Fancy—fade as light before the day!

A Prison Scene.

I.

THE clouds are hast'ning day's decline,—their mighty folds are spread
Above our island's giant frame, like palls that wrap the dead;
And gleams of light fall faintly down, and quickly fade away,
Like flushes on the cheeks of youth that herald life's decay.

II.

Within a gloomy prison-cell a gallant youth appears,—
The hope of Freedom's bright up-rise illumed his path of years.

Young Emmett dared to love our isle, and love
    engender'd zeal ;
He pledg'd his life in Erin's cause to work the
    Nation's weal.

III.

Adown through grated windows dim the strug-
    gling daylight falls,—
The gloom is spreading round the cell—it creeps
    along the walls ;
And dark the fate that hovers near, yet Robert's
    heart is warm,—
He hopes, he prays that Freedom's barque may
    weather through the storm.

IV.

But hark ! the iron bolts are drawn—the door is
    opened wide,
And soon a maiden, meek and sad, is standing
    by his side.
Adown her cheeks the pearly tears in ceaseless
    streamlets flow ;—
Her heart has burst beyond its bounds beneath
    a weight of woe !

V.

"Ah, Sarah! fondest, dearest one! my days of
    joy have fled;
The breast that bears a double love will soon be
    with the dead;
The heart that beat in happy times for you and
    Erin's isle,
Will soon be still, and feel no more a loving
    woman's smile.

VI.

"But O! when death has seal'd my eyes, and
    quench'd the vital flame,
Remember Robert through the years, and guard
    the martyr's fame.
And when amidst the happy scenes thy lover
    lov'd so well,
Think, think while living how he lov'd, and
    loving how he fell!

VII.

"Aye, fell! but not where Erin's flags midst
    gallant columns wave!
A martyr in my country's cause, I find an early
    grave.

But weep not! sweeter far to die in Freedom's
    blesséd cause,
Than live a slave beneath the sword that dire
    Oppression draws!

VIII.

"If cowards slight this noble cause, and mock
    my brief career,
Subdue thy throbbing, bursting heart, and dry
    the gushing tear,
And raise thy gentle voice awhile thy lover's
    fame to save;—
O! bless the cause of Fatherland,—give honor
    to the brave!

IX.

"Farewell! my life is dwindling fast, as fades
    the light of day;
We'll meet again, to part no more, in regions far
    away:—
Above the skies, beyond the stars, where tyrants
    ne'er can dwell—
Fond treasure! dearer far than life! my Sarah,
    fare thee well."

X.

One mighty sigh of grief up-swells, as swells the troubled tide ;
One moment more of deepest woe, and Sarah leaves his side,
But through the lapse of stormy years no foeman dare assail
The name of Emmett — Freedom's child — the pride of Innisfail!

Glendalough.

I.

GLEN of the Lakes! I hail thee with emotion—
　Long-sighed-for object of the poet's soul!
A pilgrim-bard presents his heart's devotion
　Beside the hills where Avon's waters roll;
And sweetly o'er me steals a happy feeling
　That thou art one I oft beheld before.
The hazy curtains seem to rise, revealing
　The long-sought beauties of thy magic shore!

II.

The silv'ry lakes! what solemn awe around them,
　Embosom'd safely midst the mountains brown!
The heathy cliffs, the waving forests bound them;
　Lugduff, the giant, proudly looketh down.

The Summer sun at mid-day softly peepeth
 Adown the heather, o'er the shadow'd streams.
The gloomy lake awhile in silence sleepeth,
 Then wakes and smiles amidst the sunny beams!

III.

So grand, so solemn seems the silence reigning
 Across the glen in Summer's sweetest hour,
That Nature, weari'd, here in peace remaining
 Awhile, is slave to Slumber's witching pow'r.
She scarcely breathes beside the streamlet sighing,
 Beneath the pines that guard the sobbing lake,
Till Autumn leaves, beside the waters lying,
 With rustling voices bid the sleepers wake!

IV.

A home was here for sainted hermit glowing
 With burning love and wondrous faith divine!
A calm retreat for youth in virtue growing,
 Where Nature's God could have a fitting shrine.

And so the lakes, through brightest golden ages,
   Reflected forms of Erin's sainted men,
And while they live in grand historic pages,
   St. Kevin's works will speak amidst the glen!

V.

They stand majestic—ruined churches lowly,
   Whose mould'ring porches creeping ivy climbs.
The prelates, princes, hermits meek and holy,
   Rest 'neath the Cross that tells of better times.
And grandest sight! "the pillar-tow'r" that telleth
   Of glories gone amidst the gloom of Time;
For though no more the abbey-bell out-swelleth,
   The voiceless ruins tell their tale sublime!

VI.

Unnumber'd legends—quaint, and sweet, and tender,
   Are still preserv'd amidst the gloomy glen
Of Kevin's love—the peasant's kind defender,
   The friend and father dear to suff'ring men.

Ah, happy hours! Alas! too soon departed!
    When seated nigh the lake with friends so dear,
I heard of Kevin, kind and tender-hearted,
    And felt I had some kindred spirits near!

A LEGEND OF ST. KEVIN.

In the days when good Saint Kevin—filled with
    thoughts of God and heaven—
    Rais'd those lovely churches seven, midst the
        mountain-girdled glen;
When the hammers' sounds up-swelling, echoed
    through the hermit's dwelling,
    Sweetly ringing, gladly telling of the stalwart
        working-men.
Strongest son of honest labor, fit to wield the
    sledge or sabre,
        Was the gallant Phelim then.
Soon, too soon he left the sun-light, ne'er to see
    the earth again!

In the grave where shamrock creepeth, there
    the gallant worker sleepeth—
    There a widow'd woman weepeth, wailing
        wildly o'er the dead;

But at eve she sinketh slowly on her couch so
    lone and lowly,
  And she prays, with spirit holy, that, as joys
    of earth have fled,
She may rest and be forgiven, midst the golden
    halls of heaven,—
    She may see the field outspread,
Where her husband's spirit walketh forth from
    dwellings of the dead!

Ere the dawn her death is knelling, where the
    Avon's waves were swelling,
  And two infants' cries are telling of the births
    that came in woe.
Ah! the twins are now forsaken! ne'er their
    mother shall awaken!
  To the Spirit-land she's taken, and her babes
    are left below.
But the loss Saint Kevin heareth—by the couch
    the Saint appeareth;
    Soon he bears them o'er the snow,
To his cell beneath the mountains where the
    Avon's waters flow!

Kevin thinks of Him who feedeth ev'ry mortal
    thing that breatheth;

Surely, surely now he needeth aid from God
   for orphans young !
So hastes along the heather, through the snowy,
   stormy weather,
  To the rocks that stand together near the
   chapel's holy wall.
O'er the rock he bendeth lowly, on the rock he
   striketh slowly,
     And the iron mallets fall,—
Till a mighty stony basin stands beside the
   mountains tall !

Then he prays that at the dawning, 'neath the
   forest's frosted awning,
  By the caves so grimly yawning o'er the
   mountain-shadow'd lake,
Bounding deer may nimbly hasten to the mighty
   rocky basin,
  From their store of milk to place in some for
   orphans wanting aid ;
That the fawns may gladly spare it, that the
   lovely babes may share it,
     Nor the Saint be still afraid
That the orphan twins might wither in his cell
   beside the glade.

When the yellow dawn is breaking, lo! the
    shining deer awaking,
  Soon the mountain-bed forsaking, nimbly
    bound they down the hill.
With a sparkling glance of pleasure, pour they
    forth the milky treasure,
  Nor with miser's stinted measure, till the rocky
    bowl o'erflows,
And the twins grow daily stronger, till they
    need the milk no longer :
    Such their Heavenly Father's will.
This the lonely Irish legend that is told of Kevin
    still !

VII.

Glen of the Lakes! farewell! perhaps forever!
  Thy countless beauties fade in mist away ;
But oh! can shades of time from me dissever
  The sweet remembrance of that Summer day?
No! no! for oft, beside the prairies dwelling,
  My fancy leads me o'er the ocean waves,
To giant hills, where Avon's stream is swelling—
  To peasants' homes and hermits' holy caves !

Elegy on my Sister.

I.

O DREARY task! to send my thoughts along
In measur'd language while my soul is sad!
To try to sing a mourning, requiem song
Of her who ever made my spirits glad!

II.

Of her whose smile had ever on me beam'd,
And fill'd my heart, enkindled it with love.
Of her who ever to my fancy seem'd
An angel sent from heaven's court above!

III.

How can my heart still throb within my breast,
When mighty sorrow dwells within its core?
The voice that cheer'd it is, alas! at rest!
The loving eyes will never move it more!

IV.

In early youth she seem'd a child of God ;
    She lov'd the temple's sacred, calm retreat.
Unknown, unnotic'd mid the crowd she trod,
    While love lent swiftness to her weari'd feet.

V.

Her love ! the love that mounts unto the skies,
    That finds its rest when death removes the veil
That spreads across poor sinful mortals' eyes,
    And gives an answer to its long appeal.

VI.

Like a bright flow'r she rose before my eyes,
    And twin'd the tendrils round my youthful heart,
And as she grew she pointed toward the skies,
    And seem'd to say, "Dear brother ! we must part !"

VII.

O such a flow'r ! so lovely and so chaste,
    Could never flourish on this wicked earth !
The lily, blooming o'er the desert waste,
    Will wither soon, and soon again take birth.

VIII.

And she is gone! and naught of her remains
    Save but the mem'ry of her pious deeds,
As dear flow'rs fragrance on the desert plains
    Still hovers 'round amidst the faded weeds!

IX.

Beneath the shadow of the lofty tow'r
    Where great O'Connell's mould'ring body lies,
There is the dust of that beloved flow'r—
    And snapp'd, alas! are dear fraternal ties!

X.

The cross that crowns the great, majestic pile
    Is often shadow'd on her grassy mound.
The roaring tempest seems to rest awhile,
    And pass in silence o'er the sacred ground!

XI.

Peace to her ashes! pray'rs shall oft arise
    To her dear soul, although it reigns above.
Although rejoicing far beyond the skies,
    Her soul is happy in her Saviour's love.

XII.

Yet shall we pray at morning, noon, and eve,
   And beg her soul may soon be with her king.
Resign'd and hopeful, never shall we grieve,
   But feel the joy that hopes of heaven bring!

Commemoration Day.

I.

THE voice of war is hushed, the struggle o'er!
   And blessed peace is smiling once again!
The hum of trade is heard from shore to shore,
   That girds our Nation midst the mighty main.
The peasant pioneers, on hill and plain,
   O'erthrow the forest giants, plough the soil;
And mankind hails the new and happy reign
   Of empire gained by brave and honest toil—
   A prouder, nobler prize than victor's gory spoil.

II.

The storm has ceased—the clouds have passed
    away—
The fratricidal feuds are buried deep;
With equal light the Summer smiles to-day
    O'er silent graves where friend and foeman
    sleep,
Where widows, orphans, oft at even' weep!
    Away with grief, and sing the soldiers' fame,
And on their tombs the flow'ry garlands heap;
    Nor whisper aught of censure, scorn, or
    blame
    Beside the silent tomb that bears a "rebel's"
    name!

III.

In peace beside each other sleep the brave,
    And "dust to dust" they pass to Mother
    Land!
The earth that forms the soldier's lowly grave
    Is native soil, for which they drew the brand,
And fought and fell amidst a brother-band.
    Then place the laurel over ev'ry tomb,

And scatter flow'rs around with lavish hand—
  No soldier's grave shall cast a shade of gloom,
  But like a garden-bed with flow'rs of May shall bloom!

IV.

And flock around, ye men of foreign climes.
  Who found a refuge 'neath the Nation's shield,
And paid, with grateful hearts, in darkest times,
  The debt you owed, upon the battle-field.
In noble deeds to none you wish to yield,—
  Then gather 'round and sing the soldiers' praise
Whose love for freedom with their life was seal'd;
  And once again the Starry Banner raise
  Above the gallant dead who fell in other days!

Godless Teachings.

I.

THE children growing up in boyhood's prime,
  Are young recruits for dang'rous days preparing—
For struggles ever on the path of Time,
  Where cares are great, and human foes are daring;
Where worldly wiles beset the toiler's way,
  Like weeds around the rising plant entwining;
And foes of Truth the tempting fruit display—
  The serpent's craft and darkest guile combining.

II.

The weapon strongest in the ceaseless strife—
  The armor guarding hearts that know no terror—
That carves a path amidst the maze of life,
  And guards the young beside the gulf of error,

Is Learning—subject to Religion's sway—
  Like purest stream that flows from sparkling
    fountain,
Constrain'd within its proper course to stay,
  When rolling down the high and furrow'd
    mountain.

III.

'Tis vain to learn the gifts of Mother Earth—
  To scan the motions made by starry legions,
And hear no word of Him who gave them birth,
  And mark'd their path amidst the cloudy
    regions!
To search the deepest depths of Learning's
    mine,
  No light of faith your feeble steps directing,
Is labor lost! the mind's unbroken shrine
  Is dark, indeed, Religion's aid neglecting.

IV.

My country's sons! when bigot tyrants sought
  To kill the faith your fathers fondly cherish'd;
The holy priest, the man who science taught,
  Beneath the sword of persecution perish'd.

Yet altars rose within the mountain caves,
    And Learning's stream was guarded midst afflictions,
And priest and teacher sunk to honor'd graves
    Amidst a people's grateful benedictions.

v.

To-day of Learning's poison'd draught beware,
    That comes from foes — our country's base deceivers!
O guard *the lambs!*—your little ones—with care,
    The poison'd cup would make them *unbelievers!*
Your *Shepherds'* call rings o'er the sainted land;
    Their voice of warning woke our faithful Nation.
Avoid the gifts that fill the bigot's hand,
    And save your sons from "Godless Education."

Doctor Yore.

(A philanthropic Priest, beloved by the citizens of Dublin. He died in that city in the month of February, 1864.)

I.

DEAR stricken Isle! amidst thy countless woes
  One gleam of hope still lights the path of years;
One holy love amidst thy children grows,
  Unchang'd by want, unchill'd by earthly fears;
Sweet holy hope, and love for him who cheers
  The drooping soul with gifts that God bestows.
Dear priests of Erin! Heav'n's anointed peers!
  Though Celtic hearts have felt unnumber'd throes,
  For you the light of love undimm'd forever glows.

II.

Alas! another guiding star has set!
    Another "Soggarth" gone forevermore,
Whose loss our island cannot soon forget—
    Her sainted son—the venerated Yore.
Let pray'rs arise throughout our sea-girt shore,
    Let pious joy destroy each vain regret;
Angelic bands his happy spirit bore
    To realms of bliss, where, free from Adam's debt,
    That faithful Irish priest his Lord at length has met.

III.

The people's priest! How sad they seem to-day,
    The loving poor, who watch'd his sunny smile,
And felt his aid upon their rugged way,
    And knew that heart that knew not human guile,
That throbb'd for God, for man, for native Isle!
    Who gave the sadden'd blind a holy ray,*

---

* The allusions are to Dr. Yore's connection with "St. Mary's Asylum for Industrious Blind," "Catholic Society for Support of Deaf and Dumb," "St. Vincent de Paul's Orphanage," &c.

To cheer their hearts, dispel each worldly wile
  That sought to lead their tott'ring steps astray,
  And make the child of God the pros'lytizer's prey!

IV.

Ah! silent children! little "mutes," who ne'er
  Rejoic'd a mother's heart with vocal sound,
Nor lisp'd to Heav'n a child's sweet, simple pray'r,
  When ev'ning cast its heavy shades around—
You grieve to-day, for fond affection bound
  Your heart to him who banish'd dark despair,
Through whom asylum, blessed by Heav'n, you found,
  Where, led by truth, and free from worldly care,
  Your youthful, pious souls their thanks to God declare.

V.

Ye little orphans! stay the tears that flow
  Adown your cheeks as once they fell before;
Your second father leaves you here below,
  But lives above, his earthly labors o'er.

Strive, strive like him to gain that priceless
store
  Of blessings bright which midst this earth oft
  grow;
Your pastor's field a glorious harvest bore.
  Then youth go forth—with hopeful spirit sow
  Seeds like that godly father's, midst this world
  of woe.

Dalkey.

Near where the ocean rolls its boist'rous
tide,
Tow'rd fair Eblana from the Eastern side,—
Near where Killiney lifts its rugged form
High tow'rd the skies, nor fears the wintry
storm:
Near where the billows loudly, madly roar,
When sweeping swiftly past "the Colamore,"
The ancient town of lovely Dalkey stands—
The fairest spot amidst the Irish lands.

In ancient times, while Erin yet was free,
Ere Saxon despots cross'd the foaming sea,—
When Irish monarchs held the Irish throne,
And plac'd their hopes in Irish hands alone,
Here mighty chiefs, midst splendor, pass'd their days,
And lords and peasants heard the bardic lays
Which told of wars between some Danish band
And hardy clansmen of our Father-land.

Oft did the walls with boist'rous laughter sound
That now in ruins seem to seek the ground.
Oft on Killiney did the signals burn
That told the clansmen of the chief's return.
Oft through old Dalkey march'd a gallant band,
The pride and glory of our Celtic land;
And tow'rd his home the stalwart peasant trod,
With cheerful mien—in peace with man and God.

Those days have pass'd on Time's deceitful wing;
No more these walls with joyous laughter ring;
No more the strains of golden harps swell high,
To tell that chiefs of noble blood are nigh.

Yet Dalkey still retains its ancient fame,
And lovely scenes are blended with its name.
For though the tyrant since has robb'd our lands,
And on our treasures laid destructive hands—
Though times of want and woe have pass'd since
    then,
Though dead, long ago, are the warrior-men,
Though long in ruins have those castles stood—
Still, still they stand her for the country's good,
And Nature dwells here as in days of yore,
And spreads her charms around the rocky shore.

Here poets still may revel in delight,
As 'round they gaze on ev'ry charming sight,
Or wandering down by rugged "Colamore,"
They see the billows dash against the shore,
And hear the ocean roaring far away,
Where mighty vessels leap amidst the spray.

Here Essex landed with his Saxon band,
When first he hasten'd to enslave our land.
And English war-ships rode on yonder tide,
Where naught but small boats on the waters
    glide.

Here English soldiers landed warlike store,
With many an oath and many a brutal roar,
And dragg'd the cannon up the rugged strand
To slay the men of this old Irish land.

See yonder mansion stretching toward the sea,
Remote and peaceful and from danger free.
No noise is heard except the roaring waves,
And light wind sighing through the rocky caves.
No shout arises here the live-long day,
Save when the sea-gull sweeps upon his prey.

Now on the beach the loaded fish-boat lies,
While hardy fishers soon divide the prize.
Or at the mid-day—free from grief or pain,
The old men tell of perils on the main,
And speak of fights they had in other years
With murd'rous crews of flying privateers ;
Or tell of smugglers sailing o'er the main,
With costly goods from France or lovely Spain
And others listen, though they don't forget
To mend the small sails or the broken net :—
Such sights are seen at rugged Colamore,
Where mighty billows leap against the shore.

On Summer-days I've sat on yonder hill,—
The winds at rest and Nature calm and still.
Upon the heath I've read of Rome and Greece,
The fate of nations and the sweets of peace.
Oft I have thought how sweet 'twould be for those
Long years engag'd against their country's foes,
Tired of the battle and the long campaign,
Here to retire and dwell in yonder plain.

Cross "Dalkey-Hill," or on its summit stand,
And gaze afar upon the verdant land,—
Toward where "The Scalp" and Wicklow Hills arise,
Where "Sweet Ovoca" 'tween the mountains lies,
And where "the Dargle" sweeps amidst the hills,
Where rocks resound with music of the rills.
And nearer still, Shangana's plain is seen,
With pleasant cots, and waving meadows green.
There snowy sheep and lowing cattle graze—
There sit the shepherds in the Summer-days.

Dalkey.

Let others boast of homes beyond the main,
In sunny France, in orange-bearing Spain ;
Where Alps are clad in everlasting snow ;
Where lakes abound, where sunny waters flow,
Or where the rivers sweep through orange-groves ;
Where Rhone's wild water by the mountain roves ;
Where Switzer-peasants tend the fleecy flocks,
And chase the chamois o'er the shelving rocks ;
Or yet again where cascades cast the spray
Midst rosy banks, and leap about all day.
Yes! even talk of homes along the Rhine,
And lovely walks amidst the trellis'd vine.
All, all would vanish from my glowing mind,
And leave one thought — one longing wish behind—
To live, to die amidst each lovely scene
That decks Old Dalkey like a bridal-queen !

Our University.

Written on the occasion of laying the corner-stone of the Catholic University of Ireland, in 1862.

I.

REJOICE, ye Celts! whate'er your lot may be,
  If still the sparks of faith your bosoms fire,
If still ye long for homes and altars free,
  And seek for hope to guide each dear desire;
Rejoice! for lo, our burning feuds expire
  When Erin's prelates wake "the sainted land."
And though each year some stars of hope retire,
  And sorrows break, like waves along the strand—
  Still, still our darling isle the tempests will withstand!

II.

Oh, gladsome sight! oh, proudest, brightest day
  That dawn'd for years upon our slighted isle!
When stalwart thousands march'd in strong array,
  'Neath Irish skies in Summer's sunny smile,
To show their front against their ruler's guile,
  To tell the world that Ireland's faithful race,
Though poor, dejected, wakes to life awhile,
  Resolv'd to give to learning hallow'd place—
  A home where Faith shall reign which man can ne'er deface!

III.

Methought, as onward roll'd the human stream:
  The marshall'd force of thirty thousand men—
That sight of wonder was a happy dream
  Of olden times by wooded hill and glen.
To hear the tramp, the stirring strains, as when
  The Celtic clans as victors left the field,

Would move the faintest heart to hope again
   That men who long in vain for rights appeal'd,
   And now behold their strength, will ne'er to tyrants yield.

IV.

Ah! long ago our island's wondrous fame
   As Learning's home was midst the nations spread,
Till Europe, startled, echo'd Erin's name,
   And thirsting students towards her temples sped,
Where learned Saints the lamp of science fed.
   Ah! then no bigot laws our country bound,
But Learning, Truth, one golden glory shed;
   "The Isle of Scholars" then was holy ground,
   Where Science honor'd God, and Arts a refuge found!

V.

Alas! in evil hour the tyrants came,
   And sorrows brooded o'er our ruin'd state;
The English edicts smother'd Learning's flame:
   The vilest serfdom seem'd our fathers' fate;

But soon, despite the tyrants' hellish hate,
  They nourish'd Knowledge in their mountain-
    caves,
Where priests and teachers midst their people
    sate—
  An out-law'd band, who sunk to honor'd
    graves,
  Or wept in exile homes beyond the distant
    waves.

VI.

Oh, joyous thought! our fathers' faith survives,
  · And love for learning stirs our people still.
And struggling Erin—hopeful—boldly strives
  To make her rulers own a Nation's will.
May Faith and Science once again fulfil
  Their happy task in Irish classic halls;
May Erin's cause her future students thrill,
  Till youth shall stand where Faith or country
    calls,
  And strive to break each bond that weakens
    or enthralls!

Ode on Washington's Birth-Day,
1872.
Delivered at the Inauguration of the Catholic Hall, Leavenworth, Kansas.

I.

WE ope the gates of Knowledge,
    We hail the eager throng
That surges onward toward the shrine
    Of orat'ry and song.
We bless the star of Liberty
    That sheds a light around,
And we pray, on this day,
    That no despot may be found
To enslave the soul, debase the mind !—
    That no despot may be found.

II.

O, noble chief ! whose mem'ry
    A grateful race recalls,—
Whose name should blaze in starry light
    Around our humble walls !

Thy hand, that struck Oppression down,
  The wounds of faction bound.
So we pray, on this day,
  That no despot may be found
To enslave the soul, debase the mind!—
  That no despot may be found.

III.

No fitter day to open
  The doors of Learning's hall.
No better time to raise the heart,
  And olden thoughts recall,—
Than now, when o'er the continent
  Our father's praises sound.
And we pray, on this day,
  That no despot may be found
To enslave the soul, debase the mind!—
  That no despot may be found.

IV.

Our mighty country's Father
  No bigot feeling knew.
He struck "for homes and altars free"—
  He left these gifts for you.

So here, whate'er our faith may be,
  His praises we shall sound,
As we pray, on this day,
  That no despot may be found
To enslave the soul, debase the mind!—
  That no despot may be found.

V.

O! blessed light of Freedom!
  The suff'rer looks to thee,
And seeks thee from his distant home
  Beyond the stormy sea.
And here, to-night, with grateful hearts,
  Thy champion's praises sound,
As we pray, on this day,
  That no despot may be found
To enslave the soul, debase the mind!—
  That no despot may be found.

Winter in Town.

I.

AH! the day is dull and dreary—
    Dreary as the night;
For the sky above is clouded,
And the glorious sun is shrouded,
And the heart grows sad and weary,
    Longing for the light.
Ah! my heart is sad and weary!
    Dreary as the night.

II.

Dismal show'rs for ever patter
    On the walks below,
And they strike my windows madly,
And they trickle down them sadly,
And, with wildest din and clatter,
    Mimic rivers flow.
Thus my spirits, like the streamlets,
    Gloomy every flow!

III.

In my lofty study sitting,
    High above the town,
Gaze I, through the falling showers,
To the home amidst the bowers,
Where the sunny beams seem flitting
    Ever up and down.
Ah! the beams are on the hill-side
    Flitting up and down.

Prologue.

Spoken on St. Patrick's Day, at au Entertainment given by the "Irish-American Dramatic Club."

HAIL to the exiles far from Erin's shore!
    Who love the land their fathers lov'd of yore;
Who love the isle, that rests amidst the waves,
Where daisies grow above their mothers' graves.
Hail to them all! To-day their mem'ry roams
In fancy back to Ireland's happy homes;

To hills whose breasts are clad in garb of green,
Where yellow moss with shamrock-leaves is seen,—
Where laughing children, agéd men to-day,
Bend lowly down, and bending seem to pray,—
While seeking midst the grass a gem as fair
To Irish eyes as em'ralds "rich and rare."
Ah! many a time we've heard our fathers tell
Of mossy banks beside a bubbling well,
Where greenest shamrock met their eager gaze
On "Patrick's morning" in their boyhood's days,
And how they pluck'd and plac'd it on their breast,
To show they loved the faith of Patrick best,—
The faith that flourish'd midst the nation's woes,
That, trampled down, like shamrock, proudly rose.
Hail to the exiles! in our festive hall
We meet, the young, the old—Hibernians all!
"Sons of Hibernians"—such the name we bear,
For Irish parents claim us as their care.
We stand before you, eager to essay
To cheer your hearts on Patrick's happy day,
To wake the merry laugh and happy smile
In exil'd sons of Erin's suff'ring isle.

Prologue.

Upon this stage Hibernians' sons will come
And sound the shrilly fife and rolling drum.
And sing the songs of Erin—"Music's queen!"
And act a part in drama's moving scene.
Great is our wish, our effort to succeed,—
If yet we fail, O "take the will for deed."
The curtain moves! I boldly now announce, sir,
The farce of "Box and Cox and Mrs. Bouncer."
And though no smile light up your Celtic faces,
When "Pierce O'Hara" talks of Irish races;
Yet when old "Bouncer" speaks to "Box," the
    printer,
If ev'ry heart is cold as ice of Winter,
You must dissolve, and laugh, and grow right
    merry,
And feel as frisky as young kids in Kerry.
I'll merely add this adage to our greeting—
"The pudding's proof is always in the eating."

SONGS.

♣

The Wicklow Vales.

Air—"*Limerick is Beautiful.*"

OH! brightly beams the Summer sun
    On fair lands far away;
  A garb of green the valleys wear,
    Where silv'ry streamlets stray.
But boyhood's home I'll ne'er forget,
    Though dark my fate may be—
Where'er I roam, my Irish home,
    The Wicklow Vales for me.
Where'er I roam, my Irish home,
    The Wicklow Vales for me.

There's music in the leafy woods,
    And mid the rocky hills—
The rolling tones that follow fast
    The leaping, rippling rills.

And sunshine dances round our door
　　At mid-day, wild with glee,
And proudly stand the mountains grand!
　　The Wicklow Vales for me.
And proudly stand the mountains grand!
　　The Wicklow Vales for me.

Amidst those hills the steel was heard,
　　And music's martial strain,
When patriots sought to make our isle
　　"A nation once again."
The outlaw bold, like eagle wild,
　　On mountain's brow was free—
Oh! Freedom's home! where'er I roam,
　　The Wicklow hills for me.
Oh! Freedom's home! where'er I roam,
　　The Wicklow hills for me.

Ah! sorrows fall like mountains' shades
　　O'er brightest scenes of earth,
Yet hope remains amid these plains
　　To hail the morrow's birth.
And gladly glides the Winter's night,
　　Mid scenes of mirth and glee—

Where'er I roam, my mountain home,
  The Wicklow Vales for me.
Where'er I roam, my mountain home,
  The Wicklow Vales for me.

Let others boast of happy homes
  In fair lands far away,
My love for thee shall never fade,
  Where'er my footsteps stray.
Dear Wicklow! Home of loving hearts,
  My mountain nurse, Machree!
No vales can e'er with thine compare,
  The Wicklow Vales for me.
No vales can e'er with thine compare,
  The Wicklow Vales for me.

The Dance.

AIR—"*Billy O'Rourke.*"

T HE Summer sun is laughing down,
    And o'er the heather glancing—
We'll haste away ere close of day
    To join the peasants dancing
Beneath the ivy-clothed trees
    That guard the farmer's dwelling,
And softly shake their leafy bells,
    While music's strains are swelling—
We'll haste away, we'll haste away,
    Along the scented heather;
We'll join the merry peasant band,
    And "trip the sod" together.

From silent glen, from mossy moor,
    From cabin lone and dreary,
They come—the *friezed* and *hooded* band,
    With spirits never weary.

The Dance.

With hearts so light that sorrows ne'er
  Can break their sense of pleasure—
The Irish heart that laughs at care
  Is bless'd with brightest treasure.
We'll haste away, we'll haste away,
  Along the scented heather;
We'll join the merry peasant band,
  And "trip the sod" together.

The stars will peep amidst the trees,
  Their light with moonbeams blended,
Before the music dies away,
  Before the dance is ended.
And joke and laughter, wild and free,
  Ring round the farmer's dwelling,
And lithesome limbs keep measur'd time
  Where Irish airs are swelling.
We'll haste away, we'll haste away,
  Along the scented heather;
We'll join the merry peasant-band,
  And "trip the sod" together.

As long as happy Irish hearts
  Are throbbing through the Nation—

As long as Irish exiled sons
   Are found on God's creation—
As long as music's thrilling strains
   Can wake a sweet emotion,
We'll save the custom of our sires
   At home and o'er the ocean.
We'll haste away, we'll haste away,
   Along the scented heather ;
We'll join the merry peasant-band,
   And "trip the sod" together.

My Lovely Isle, Adieu !

AIR—"*Shule Aroon.*"

I.

AWAY from Erin's lovely shore
   My weary heart with grief is sore,—
Alas ! I'll never see thee more !
   My lovely isle, adieu !
Far, far, far from thee
We sail away on the stormy sea.
Ah ! could I sleep on the rolling deep,
   And cease to dream of you !

II.

Ah! oft in happy times I've stray'd
Thro' meadows green and forests' shade
From father's cot beside the glade,—
    But now, old home, adieu!
Far, far, far from thee
We sail away on the stormy sea.
Ah! could I sleep on the rolling deep,
    And cease to dream of you!

III.

They say the land is rich to-day
Where wild Missouri's waters stray
Midst prairies boundless, far away.
    Ah! fairer land, adieu!
Far, far, far from thee
We sail away on the stormy sea.
Ah! could I sleep on the rolling deep,
    And cease to dream of you!

IV.

No riches gain'd on foreign shore
Can e'er my youthful joys restore,

Can steal my heart from thee, asthore!
    My lóvely isle, adieu!
Far, far, far from thee
We sail away on the stormy sea.
Ah! could I sleep on the rolling deep,
    And cease to dream of you!

Gazing Westward.

WHEN the shades of eve are blending
    Where the fleecy clouds have roll'd;
When the ruddy sun descending
    Tips the mountain-tops with gold;
When the weary soul is sinking,
    Like the setting sun, to rest,—
Then of olden times I'm thinking,
    Gazing fondly tow'rd the West!

Far beyond the forests olden,
    Where the shadows creep to-night;
Far beyond the mountains golden,
    Gilt with day's declining light;

Gazing Westward.

Far beyond the billows foaming,
   O'er the ocean's troubled breast,
Tow'rd the past my heart is roaming,
   Gazing fondly tow'rd the West!

Yet I gaze, though tears are gushing,
   Though my throbbing heart is sore;
Yet I stand, though onward rushing
   Roll the scenes I'll see no more.
Shadows gather gloom around me;
   Happy sounds disturb my rest,
Rudely breaking bonds that bound me,
   Gazing fondly tow'rd the West.

Yet in Fancy's pow'r I wander,
   By the olden paths at eve;
O'er the vanish'd years I ponder;
   For the stricken Isle I grieve.
Yet I watch for day's awaking—
   Though the sun has sunk to rest—
For the light of Freedom breaking
   O'er the dim and distant West!

O, Lovely Land!

O LOVELY land! where'er I roam,
   I oft will think of thee!
Where'er I fix my future home,
   Whate'er my lot may be.
If midst the shades of forest trees
   Beneath a foreign sky,
My thoughts shall speed across the seas
   To where thy valleys lie.

Could I forget to sing thy praise
   Thou beautiful and fair?
Could I forget my early days,
   Amidst my worldly care,
That I have spent upon thy breast—
   Thy lovely breast of green,
Thou beauteous daughter in the West—
   Atlantic's peerless queen?

All beautiful but sad art thou—
   A slave amidst the free!
Enchain'd and lone thou sittest now,
   Encircl'd by the sea.
Like widow fair in gloomy weeds,
   Thou smilest mid thy tears—
Thou hardy nurse of gallant deeds
   In long departed years!

Thy sons oft sought to break thy chain,
   To raise thy drooping head,
But still a slave thou dost remain,
   And hope from thee has fled.
Yet soon, perhaps, thou wilt arise,
   Like one from out the tomb,
Like sun-light bursting from the skies,
   Chasing the Nation's gloom!

Hunting Song.

Air—*"Shilly Shally."*

TRUMPETS sounding, horses bounding,—
   O, how happy seems the day!
When we sally from the valley,
   Chasing Reynard far away.
Far away, while through the mountains
   Ring the notes we love to hear,—
Music sweet to happy hunters,
   Made by hounds in wild career!

Downward dashing streams are flashing—
   Scarlet streams of hunters bold!
Swiftly going where are flowing
   Mountain torrents uncontroll'd.
Loose the reins and spur the charger,—
   Gallant steed we've won our way!
Rush again through glen and meadow;
   Boldly hold the lead to-day.

Still careering, nothing fearing,
    Now we're rushing through the vale—
Glen of glory! fam'd in story!
    Lovely glen of wild Imael!
Up the rugged, rocky mountains,
    Where the "mountain-fox" is seen.
O! I love your brow of boldness,
    Tow'ring heights of old Kaigeen!

Naught shall ever rudely sever
    Happy thoughts of long ago,
Spent in racing, wildly chasing,
    Where "the Greece" and "Slaney" flow.
Hark! again the trump is sounding!
    See! the dogs are rushing round.
Huntsman's whoop—the wild "you-youp,"
    Tells that Reynard's "run to ground."

The Friends whom I Loved Long Ago.

Air—"*The Beautiful Maid of my Soul.*"

AWAY midst our Irish hills,
   My heart and my thoughts are to-day,
By the banks of the streamlets that dance
   To the Emerald meadows away.
But darkness comes down through the glen;
   The rivers, too, wail as they flow,
For I miss those that brightened the scene—
   The friends whom I lov'd long ago.

Beside the old castle walls,
   Where ivy is green as of old,
Have I sat in the shade in the eve,
   When the heavens their banners unroll'd,
And listen'd to tales of the past,—
   Of Erin's dark ages of woe;
Ah! 'twas then that I valu'd them most—
   The friends whom I lov'd long ago.

Away midst the forests' wilds,
  Where roll the Missouri's dark waves,
They have sought for a refuge—a home—
  For this land is an island of slaves!
But ever they hope, midst the gloom,
  To strike yet for Erin a blow;
Ah! soon may we see them again—
  The friends whom we lov'd long ago!

The Green Flag.

Air—"*We'll Rally round the Flag.*"

Ah! our flag is in the dust now—
  The flag our fathers bore,
    Fighting to free our Mother Ireland!
And the Saxons tramp it down in
  The gallant Nation's gore,
    Fighting to free our Mother Ireland!
Why do we loiter while hope remains?
Strike for her freedom! shatter her chains!
  O! we'll rush to raise that flag, boys!
  The flag our fathers bore,
    Fighting to free our Mother Ireland!

Ah! that flag was rais'd awhile
  On the heathy mountains high,
      Calling for aid for Mother Ireland!
And though tyrants tore it down,
  We will lift it up or die,
      Fighting to free our Mother Ireland!
Swear to be faithful! pledge heart and hand!
Flock to her standard! rescue our land!
  O! we'll rush to raise that flag, boys!
    The flag our fathers bore,
      Fighting to free our Mother Ireland!

By the wrongs of many years,
  By the tombs of martyred men,
      Fighting to free our Mother Ireland!
By the shroudless paupers' graves,
  We now swear to strike again,
      Fighting to free our Mother Ireland!
Fling out the Green flag—wide let it wave;
Rush to that standard, sons of the brave!
  O! we'll bear that flag afar, boys!
    Through Erin's cruel foes,
      Fighting to free our Mother Ireland!

"God Save Old Ireland."

AIR—"*The Admiral.*"

HOW fondly now, how proudly now, the exiles' bosoms swell
With thoughts of scenes of loveliness by lake and hill and dell:
With mem'ries of the sunny hours that faded soon away,
Like golden light that gleams awhile at dawning hour of day!
And tear-drops glisten in the eyes of gallant men and true,—
The forest-oak, like fragile flow'r, oft bears the morning dew.
O native Isle! the heart distills such tribute-tears for thee!
God save Old Ireland!—struggling Ireland— Ireland o'er the sea!
God save Old Ireland!—struggling Ireland— Ireland o'er the sea!

How bravely now, how nobly now, the few and
    fearless stand—
The struggling sons in Freedom's van who work
    for mother-land!
Who dare the dungeon; face the steel; and
    mount the scaffold high.
Aye! ready now, like men of old, to bravely
    fight or die;
Oh! truly shall their mem'ries live—their gal-
    lant deeds be told,
And Allen's name shine through the years a
    burnish'd lamb of gold!
And Celtic mothers pray to heav'n their sons as
    brave may be!
God save Old Ireland!—struggling Ireland!—
    Ireland o'er the sea!
God save Old Ireland!—struggling Ireland!—
    Ireland o'er the sea!

Oh! may the swan-like dying notes of Erin's
    martyr'd braves
Be wafted far, and move the hearts of those
    beyond the waves—
The scatter'd Celts, whose discord dire has
    dimm'd our glorious green,—

May all unite in Larkin's name!—let women
 chant his *caione!*
Oh! let those hands that brush aside the noble
 soldier's tear,
Be stretch'd to those who vow revenge beside
 O'Brien's bier!
Swear, swear you'll struggle side by side to
 make your country free!
God save Old Ireland!—struggling Ireland!—
 Ireland o'er the sea!
God save Old Ireland!—struggling Ireland!—
 Ireland o'er the sea!

There's Music midst the Mountains.

Air—"*The Nenagh Boys.*"

ABOVE the blooming heather-hills,
    Along the dancing silver rills,
A joyous sound the soldier thrills—
    There's music midst the mountains!
From giant mountains' rocky throne,
The battle's blast at length is blown;
It rings the notes of "Garry-ow'n,"—
    There's music midst the mountains!
Then rouse ye up, my gallant boys!
My gallant boys! my gallant boys!
Then rouse ye up, my gallant boys!
    There's music midst the mountains!

The martial sounds: the sabres' clash,
The muskets' bang and fiery flash,
The bay'nets' charge, and thunder-crash!
    There's music midst the mountains!

With steady step, and side by side,
Descend like torrents' dashing tide,
And fight or die as heroes died!
    There's music midst the mountains!
Then rouse ye up, my gallant boys!
My gallant boys! my gallant boys!
Then rouse ye up, my gallant boys!
    There's music midst the mountains!

Oh! glory come to crown the brave
Who strike, a nation's life to save!
The laurel o'er the tomb shall wave—
    There's music midst the mountains!
A blessing come on those who stand,
A brave, united, fearless band,
To guard, to save our father-land!
    There's music midst the mountains!
Then rouse ye up, my gallant boys!
My gallant boys! my gallant boys!
Then rouse ye up, my gallant boys!
    There's music midst the mountains!

Farewell, Dear Land!

Air—"*Good-by, Sweet Heart, Good-by.*"

ALONG the glen I lov'd in childhood,
    I haste like one who flies the foe,—
By sunny brook, through silent wildwood,
    With drooping head I sadly go.
I bid a last adieu to-day
    To home and friends, whose holy spell
Still clings around me while I say,
    "Farewell, dear land, farewell!"

The sweetest hopes of youth have vanish'd,
    Like light behind the mountain's brow.
The fondest, truest friends are banish'd,
    And I am leaving Erin now.
The brave and true afar have gone,
    In foreign lands in peace to dwell.
I, too, in tears will wander on :—
    Farewell, dear land, farewell!

While yet the faintest hope was gleaming,
  I clung in love to father's home;
In darkest hour my heart kept dreaming
  A better time would surely come.
But ah! the tempest burst at last,
  And hope sunk 'neath Oppression's swell.
Dear cot! thy happy hours have pass'd!
  Farewell, dear land, farewell!

When billows roll, when westward sailing,
  My tearful eyes will turn again
To where I think the stars are paling
  Above that cot beside the glen.
Then gaze again, with beaming eyes,
  Right onward o'er the ocean's swell,
To where Columbia proudly lies:—
  Farewell, dear land, farewell!

Irish-American Brigade.

Air—"*Cruiskeen Lawn.*"

BENEATH the crested pines,
   Behold the snowy lines
Of a thousand camps with waving flags array'd—
   O! proudly there we see
   "The Green Flag" floating free
Above Old Ireland's gallant new Brigade,—
     New Brigade!
Above Old Ireland's gallant new Brigade.

   To guard "The Stripes and Stars"
   They hasten'd to the wars,
For they love the land that gave the Irish aid,
   And in the days of yore
   Bade us "welcome" to this shore.
So we'll aid her with our gallant new Brigade—
     New Brigade!
So we'll aid her with our gallant new Brigade.

"The Sun-burst" gleams to day
  Midst forests far away—
It casts a gleam of glory on each blade,
  And cheers the soldier's breast
  With mem'ries of the West—
O! these thoughts will nerve our gallant new
    Brigade!
    New Brigade!
O! these thoughts will nerve our gallant new
    Brigade!

O! may the day yet come
  When trumpets, fife, and drum
Shall sound a joyous anthem through each glade;
  A welcome back again
  To our brave, our banish'd men—
To the soldiers of our gallant new Brigade—
    New Brigade!
To the soldiers of our gallant new Brigade.

The Hurlers.

AIR—"*When I was bound Apprentice.*"

WHAT joy on Sunday ev'nings
   When down the old "boreen"
A gay "gorsoon" I hasten'd
   To join, on village green,
The hurlers young and lithesome
   Who toss'd the bounding-ball!
O! the days of yore, on the Irish Shore,
   That we never can recall!
O! the days of yore, on the Irish Shore,
   That we never can recall!

My frieze was not the finest,
   Yet little did I care;
My hat of straw and ribbons
   Was "much the worse of wear;"
But soon I flung them from me,
   And hail'd the bounding ball.

The Hurlers.

O ! the days of yore, on the Irish Shore,
   That we never can recall !
O ! the days of yore, on the Irish Shore.
   That we never can recall !

Like Celtic clans contending
   In battle's dreadful fray,
We strove for village honors
   While rang the loud hurrah
From young and old spectators
   Who watch'd the bounding ball.
O ! the days of yore, on the Irish Shore,
   That we never can recall !
O ! the days of yore, on the Irish Shore,
   That we never can recall.

Ah ! me ! what change has fallen
   Across our path since then !—
How many gay companions
   Shall never smile again !
Their path of life has ended
   By Abbey's ivy wall !
Ah ! the days of yore, on the Irish Shore,
   That we never can recall !
Ah ! the days of yore, on the Irish Shore,
   That we never can recall.

The Hurlers.

O! some are 'neath the banner
    That guards the exiles' home,
And some have drawn the sabre
    Beside the hills of Rome.
And some have fought and fallen
    Beneath Spoletto's Wall.
O! the days of yore, on the Irish Shore,
    That we never can recall!
O! the days of yore, on the Irish Shore,
    That we never can recall.

God grant that joy may visit
    Our peasants' home again,
That olden sports may cheer us
    On village green and glen;
That hopeful sons of Ireland
    May drive the bounding ball.
O! the days of yore, on the Irish Shore,
    That we never can recall!
O! the days of yore, on the Irish Shore,
    That we never can recall!

The Fiddler.

AIR—"*St. Kevin once was traveling.*"

I TRAVEL through our charming isle,
   From Bann to Sunny Cove,
And ever find a cheering smile
   Where'er I love to rove.
I cheer the homes of grief and care,
   And wild the young heart bounds,
When 'neath the roofs of peasants' cots
   My dear old fiddle sounds.

O! often in the summer time
   I've sat beneath a tree,
And play'd while laughing couples
   Smil'd pleasantly on me.
And "gorsoons" left the "hurley-goals;"
   And peasants stopp'd their ploughs,
And came to hear my fiddle's voice
   Beneath the spreading boughs.

The Fiddler.

When Winter-snows are on the ground,
   And nights are cold and drear,
Beside the blazing fire of turf
   The farmer's friends appear.
Awhile they talk of long ago,
   The happy days of yore—
I strike my fiddle!—up they jump
   And dance about the floor.

On Sunday nights the dance is held
   In some secluded spot.
O! then I think myself a King
   So happy is my lot.
The gallant youths soon gather 'round—
   They form the dancing row,—
They take their places, wheel about
   And "trip the heel and toe."

You talk of balls in palace halls,
   And boast of pleasures there,
With music of Italian bands
   You think so "rich and rare."
But give me dear old Ireland's songs
   Beside the peasant's fire,
And Irish airs for Irish jigs,—
   No better I desire.

From Far Away.

Air—"*The Honey-Moon.*"

UP! up! the day is dawning bright,
   The hills are tipp'd with purple light,
The glassy lakes are lovely sight,
      Like happy hearts at rest!
The Sun that lifts his head on high,
The gentle winds that softly sigh,
The streams that ripple laughing by—
      All tell we're in the West.

We launch our boat upon the bay,
Beneath the tow'ring mountains gray;
We gaze along the sparkling spray,
      To scenes we lov'd of old.
To where on sunny Sunday eves
We rov'd amidst the yellow leaves;
Ah! still my bounding bosom heaves
      With thoughts of bliss untold.

From Far Away.

The little school is standing still,
The homestead stands on yonder hill;
My eyes with tears of sorrow fill!
      How roll'd the past away!
And stormy tempests roll'd around
Since first I left the Irish ground.
A haven bright at last I found,
      Where Freedom's zephyrs play!

Come, brothers! ply the dripping oar,
And guide our boat to yonder shore.
I'll stand on father's land once more
      And kiss the sacred sod!
And though no mother's voice again
Can call me up the silent glen,
I'll dream awhile I'm young as when
      The shady paths I trod.

The Little Bit of Land.

Air—"*The Green Fields of America.*"

AH! tempt me not, my master, with the offer of your shining gold,
To win from me the little spot my sainted father lov'd of old,
To take from me the humble home that ne'er to me or mine was cold.
    Ah! leave me! and I'll ask no more, the little bit of land!
Ah! tell me not, to tempt me, that the gold could win a home for me,
And peace and hope and happiness beyond the distant rolling sea.
No! nothing, dearest, native Isle! could win my loving heart from thee!
    Ah! leave me, and I'll ask no more, the little bit of land!

Sure even though the yellow grain is not so rich
    as long ago,
Though darkest blight is o'er the fields where all
    the young potatoes grow ;
Though Famine's breath has wither'd men, and
    wak'd the wail of want and woe,
        Ah! leave me, and I'll ask no more, the
        little bit of land.

Before my father went to rest, in yonder grave
    beneath the trees,
He bless'd me as I wept and pray'd beside him
    on my bended knees ;
He ask'd me still to cling to home and ne'er to
    cross the stormy seas,
        He left me, and I ask no more, a little
        bit of land.

Ah, master! sure your fleecy sheep have fertile
    fields to feed upon ;
They'll never pine and die of want as died our
    brothers gaunt and wan.
The willing heart, the helping hand, the friendly
    neighbors all have gone.
        But leave me, and I ask no more, the
        little bit of land.

I'm lonely, very lonely now, but yet one hope
  my bosom thrills:
That when the iron hand of death my throbbing
  heart forever stills,
They'll lay me down in holy ground beside my
  darling Irish hills,—
    They'll give me, and I ask no more, *a
    little bit of land.*

Faithful Unto Death.

A BLESSING on the gallant heart
  That fears no human foe,
That bravely dares the stroke of fate,
  Unmov'd in weal or woe;
Who stands undaunted on the field,
  And cries with latest breath
"I glory still through good and ill,
  I'm faithful unto death.
I glory still through good and ill,
  I'm faithful unto death."

Faithful Unto Death.

A blessing on the sailor bold
    Afar from native land,
Who looks along the stormy sea,
    The tiller in his hand.
And bravely guides the bounding bark,
    Despite the tempest's breath
Midst ocean's shock, by shoal and rock,
    Still faithful unto death.
Midst ocean's shock, by shoal and rock,
    Still faithful unto death.

But O!—there's one as bold and brave
    As any heart can be;
As true as soldier midst the foes
    As sailor on the sea.
As valiant in the cause of right,
    And true to latest breath.
Kind heaven sends such gallant friends,
    Still faithful unto death.
Kind heaven sends such gallant friends,
    Still faithful unto death.

Then let the battle roll around,
    Or tempests burst above,
The bravest heart is that which throbs
    With patriotic love.

The honest son—the man that guards
   That cause to latest breath,—
And ere he dies in triumph cries,
   "I'm faithful unto death.
And ere he dies in triumph cries,
   "I'm faithful unto death."

A Green Sod from Erin.

I HAVE brought a bright treasure
   From home's holy shrine,
Where the friends who have lov'd me
   Still loving repine.
How verdant the grass is!
   How fresh is the clay!
Sweet emerald treasure
   From home far away!

Little sod!—I once found it
   Beside the old door
Where my mother caress'd me
   In sweet days of yore!

A Green Sod from Erin.

Where footsteps of childhood
    First totter'd in play.
Sweet emerald treasure
    From home far away!

Wildest storms from the mountains
    Have swept o'er it long
Yet they hurt it no more than
    A summer bird's song.
And sunlight danced o'er it
    Till ev'ning grew gray,
Sweet emerald treasure
    From home far away.

As the tears of the loved ones
    Have fallen in show'rs
O'er this green sod—memento
    Of happier hours.
So those of the exile
    Shall moisten the clay.
Sweet emerald treasure
    From home far away.

The Exile's Love.

AIR—*"My Love is like the red, red Rose.*

THE lover sings his plaintive songs,
    The soldier thrilling strains,
The shepherd tunes his shrilly pipe
    Upon the distant plains.
But sweeter far for me—my friends—
    When Summer's night is nigh
To sit beneath the forest trees
    And hear the zephyrs' sigh.

I hear them sigh, and then I think
    They come from o'er the sea,
From lovely, verdant Irish vales
    With tales of home for me.
Ah, dearest love ! my native Isle !
    My heart is all thine own !
It seems to fly to thee at eve,
    And leave me here alone !

The Exile's Love.

I think the wind that sweeps the hills
    Behind my father's home
The same that swells the vessel's sails
    And lifts the curling foam.
And bears some long-departed voice
    O'er seas from shore to shore,
To whisper through those lonely woods
    Thy name, Old Isle asthore!

Dear Ireland! while my life remains
    My love shall never die!
When fondest mem'ries come thy name
    Shall mingle with each sigh.
My dearest love! my darling isle!
    My heart is all thine own!
It seems to fly to thee at eve
    And leave me here alone!

Christmas on the Prairies.

Air—"*Tramp, Tramp.*"

SEATED here this Christmas night
  In our prairie home so bright;
Far away from lovely Erin o'er the sea;
  We will talk of other days,
  We will sing the Celtic lays,
We will swear to make our suff'ring mother free;
  High, high, high, we raise the wine-cup,
  Pledging our lives, Old Land, for thee!
    We will ne'er deny the claim
    Of our isle of olden fame—
We will never cease to strive to set her free!

  Rich and lovely lands we own
  Where the golden grain is sown,
And our countless flocks are grazing o'er the
    plains;

Yet though peace and plenty smile
Far from Erin's lovely isle,
We will ne'er forget our country, though in chains.
High, high, high, we raise the wine-cup
Pledging our lives, Old Land, for thee!
We will ne'er deny the claim
Of our isle of olden fame—
We will never cease to strive to set her free!

Gallant leaders lie to-day,
In the prisons far away,
For *the crime* of loving thee, our lovely Queen!
For they sought to strike a blow
Where the Lee and Liffey flow,
And to raise again our own beloved Green!
High, high, high, we raise the wine-cup
Pledging our lives, Old Land, to thee!
We will ne'er deny the claim
Of our isle of olden fame—
We will never cease to strive to set her free!

The Fenian Name.

Air—"*None can Love like an Irishman.*"

THE ardent Fenians proudly boast
   Their love for Erin o'er the waves,
And pant to meet the Saxon host
   In fight beside their fathers' graves.
If love for Ireland lifts them up
   Above vile faction, class, or clan
Then here's my hand! I love my land,
   And claim the name of Fenian-man!

If while they seek to set her free
   They join in bonds of trust and love
That all may faithful brothers be
   And win the smile of God above!
Nor fear the light, nor Father's gaze,
   Nor fall beneath Religion's ban.
O! here's my hand! I love my land,
   And claim the name of Fenian-man!

The Isle that bears upon its breast
    The countless temples, shrines of God ;
And where the dust of countless blest
    Lies mingled with our native sod,
Shall yet be freed by gallant men
    Who serve no faction, class or clan !
Who grasp the hand for native land
    And claim the name of Irishman !

Farewell of the Irish Maiden.

O ! MOTHER dear ! the hour has come !
    The big ship spreads her wings !
" The Starry Flag" is floating free ;
    The joyful sailor sings.
While I, thy daughter, weep and wail.
    I'll never see you more !
We sail away for New York bay,
    From Ireland's sainted shore !

I'll clasp my hands across my eyes
    When you and I must part ;
To see your anguish, Mother dear !
    Would break my bursting heart !

Farewell of the Irish Maiden.

One long, last look when out at sea,
   One pray'r for you, asthore!
When fade away the sparkling bay
   And Ireland's sainted shore!

When far away upon the deep
   I'll take "the Beads" you gave
And pray to Mary, "Mother mild,"
   Who smiles along the wave.
And beg Her smile on mother's heart
   Whom I shall see no more
When fade away the sparkling bay
   And Ireland's sainted shore!

I'll keep the little sod of earth
   You took from near our home,
And bear it near me through my life
   Wherever I may roam!
My dust shall mix with Irish earth
   When I shall be no more!
Far, far away from yonder bay
   And Ireland's sainted shore!

THE END.

www.ingramcontent.com/pod-product-compliance
Lightning Source LLC
Chambersburg PA
CBHW030259170426
43202CB00009B/809